With love for Stella Paskins, whose dad stood on the dockside and watched the *Titanic* set sail.
A.D

Text copyright © Andrew Donkin
Illustrations copyright © Linda Clark

The right of Andrew Donkin to be identified as the author of this Work and the right of Linda Clark to be identified as the illutrator of this Work has been asserted to them in accordance with the Copyright, Designs and Patenys Act 1988.

This edition first published in Great Britian in 1998 by Macdonald Young Books, an imprint of Wayland Publishers Limited

Reprinted in 1999

Typeset in 16/24pt ITC Giovanni Book

Printed and bound in Belgium by Proost International Book Production

Macdonald Young Books
61 Western Road
Hove
East Sussex
BN3 1JD

Find Wayland on the Internet
http:// www.wayland.co.uk

ISBN 0 7500 2479 8

THE UNSINKABLE
TITANIC

Andrew Donkin

Illustrated by Linda Clark

MACDONALD YOUNG BOOKS

London.
Wednesday April 10, 1912.

The events and people in this story
were real, apart from the characters
of Sarah and her mother.

Chapter 1

There seemed to be a million people in Waterloo Station that morning and they were all getting in our way.

If mother and I didn't hurry up we'd miss our train and the whole thing would be a disaster.

By the time we found it, most of the other passengers were already in their places. A porter loaded our luggage and we looked for our seats.

We had just sat down when there was a shrill whistle and the train jolted into life. The smell of the steam engine blasted in through the open window.

"How long will it take to get to Southampton?" I asked.

"About three hours. Maybe less," said mother.

Mother and I were on our way to New York to meet my father. He had been there on business for months.

We were going to sail across the Atlantic Ocean on the maiden voyage of the largest and finest ship ever built. People were excited by just the idea of it.

I had never been on a ship before and I spent the train journey imagining what it would be like.

I didn't have to wait long. As we came into Southampton dockyards, people were pressed up against the windows all along the carriage. Each of them was struggling to catch their first glimpse of the ship.

I saw her and, to be honest, I felt a little disappointed. From a distance, she looked like any other liner sitting in Southampton dockyard. However, as we slowly steamed into the docks, she got bigger and bigger.

By the time we got out of the train there was no mistake, I was impressed.

Here she was – the *Titanic*.

She stood before us, as long and as magnificent as if someone had made Buckingham Palace float. Her tall funnels sent pillars of smoke spiralling into the sky.

As we went on board we bumped into a man puffing under the weight of a double bass. He told us he was part of the ship's eight-man band and had got separated from the rest.

"Women and children first," he said with a grin, and he let us go up the gangplank before him.

On board, everything was chaotic.
All 1500 passengers and 700 new crew
members were trying to find their way
around the maze of corridors.

I thought we would never be ready in time, but at noon, six small tugs pulled us gently away from the dockside and out of the harbour. The *Titanic* powered up her huge engines and we headed out into the open sea.

Mother gave my hand a squeeze.

"Eight more days and we'll see your father," she said.

We headed back inside and started to explore our new home.

Chapter 2

Everybody got lost.

I mean everybody, even the crew. It was such a big ship you almost needed a map to find your way around.

The *Titanic* had everything you could possibly want. It was just like being in a big hotel.

There were hundreds of cabins, half a dozen different dining rooms, a library, a barber's shop, and three squash courts. There was even a gymnasium, complete with exercise bikes that didn't move.

Everything smelt brand new.

The best thing on the ship, though, was the swimming pool.

There were other children on board and I made friends with a girl called Eva. She was moving to America with her parents.

The first thing we did together was sneak into the First Class section and walk down the marble staircase pretending we owned the whole ship.

A few days into our trip, I was playing with Eva when I saw my mother waving anxiously for me to come over. She was talking to a man.

"Sarah, this is Thomas Andrews, the man who built the *Titanic*," said mother, trying to tidy up my hair as she introduced me.

"Well, I designed her," said the man, with a smile. "I had a lot of help when it came to building her."

"Mr Andrews is on board to find out what the passengers think of the ship," said mother.

I told him it was the best ship I had ever been on. (I didn't tell him it was the only one.)

We went inside to the dining room and Mr Andrews rolled out a big piece of paper across the table.

"These are the original blueprints that were used to construct her," he said.

There were sheets and sheets of them, detailing every bit of the ship down to the last nut and bolt.

"They're amazing," I said.

"I thought you'd like them. Look, this is the dining room where we're sitting right now," said Mr Andrews.

Even the tables were included on the plans. Nothing had been left to chance.

Underneath the big sheets were some smaller drawings in pen and ink. Mr Andrews saw me looking at them.

"Those are the very first sketches I ever made of her," said Mr Andrews proudly. He paused, then said, "Would you like to have one?"

He didn't have to ask twice. I pinned it up in my cabin before dinner.

Eating on board was just like being in a restaurant, except that if you watched carefully you could see the soup in your bowl ripple from side to side.

After dinner, mother and I walked around the main deck. We were thousands of kilometres from England now. The sea was calm, but it had suddenly become much colder.

The icy air sent a chill down my back and we headed inside to the warmth of our cabin.

Chapter 3

I woke up just before I hit the floor.

I had been asleep for about two hours when something bumped me out of my bed. For just a second I saw something white through the porthole window, then it was gone.

"Are you all right?" asked mother.

"Yes, but what was that? Did we hit something?"

"It was probably just a big wave," she replied.

For a while we waited inside our cabin not really knowing what to do. Then we heard people gathering in the corridor outside and mother opened the door so we could listen.

Two men were saying that it must have been a collision and someone else mentioned seeing an iceberg float by their window.

"I say, at least she's unsinkable," said a man with a very loud voice. "If we were on any other ship we might be in trouble."

It was just after midnight when
mother decided that we should
go and see what was happening for
ourselves.

"Get dressed, it's
cold out there,"
she said.

I don't think I've ever got ready so
quickly. As we were leaving, I grabbed
the drawing Mr Andrews had given me
and put it in my pocket.

Up on deck, people were wandering around. Most of them just had coats on over their pyjamas. No one really knew what was going on.

I spotted Mr Andrews and the Captain walking quickly across the deck.

Mr Andrews was as pale as if he'd seen a ghost. Mother tried to speak to him, but I don't think he really noticed her.

There was a sudden explosion of
bright white light in the sky above us
which drew a gasp from the crowd
of passengers.

"Distress rockets," said mother, and
we both realised that the ship was
really in trouble.

People crowded on to the deck from all parts of the ship now and on the far side of the deck, crew members began passing out life jackets.

Through the noise of the crowd I heard the band begin playing. They were trying to calm the passengers' nerves.

Then the first lifeboat was launched over the side of the ship. Only women and children were allowed on board, with just one male crew member to row the boat.

When they put it to sea, it was less than half full. Many people refused to get into it because they still didn't believe they were in any danger.

"Come on," said mother, grabbing my hand.

We pushed through the crowd towards where the boats were being launched. A second boat was lowered over the side, then a third.

When we got near the front of the crowd I saw that Mr Andrews was in charge of loading the fourth lifeboat. I don't think he recognised us as he helped us climb in.

"Launch it," he ordered two crew members.

They pushed the boat away from the side of the *Titanic* and began to operate the winch controls.

I looked down and realised that our tiny lifeboat was 20 metres above the sea.

"Hold on tight!" ordered mother.

I was too scared to say anything.

Without warning, there was a sudden jerk and we plunged down.

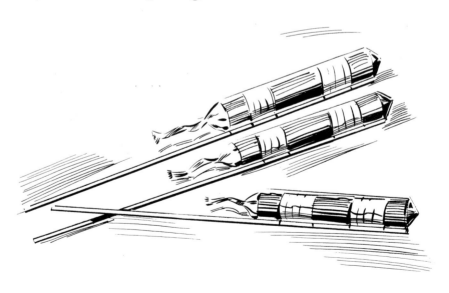

Chapter 4

The side of the ship seemed as tall as a cliff. We lurched down until we hit the water with a splash. The sea around us was as smooth as a giant pond.

As we were rowed away from the *Titanic* we could see that her nose was slowly getting lower in the water.

The impact with the iceberg had caused a long gash in her side under the waterline.

The deck of the *Titanic* was still crowded with people and every few minutes another lifeboat was launched over the side.

"Does anyone know if they sent a radio distress signal?" asked one of the ladies in our lifeboat.

"They must have," said mother. "They must have." But nobody knew for sure.

We had no torches or lights in our boat and nothing to do except watch the small figures moving around on the *Titanic's* deck. Her nose was getting lower and lower in the water.

Every now and then I could hear the sound of the band playing on. I thought of the man with the double bass.

Then I realised that they had stopped
lowering lifeboats.

"I think they've all been launched,"
said mother.

"But there's still people left on board.
Lots of people."

"There's not enough lifeboats to go
round," said mother, quietly.
She put her hand over my
eyes so I wouldn't
see, but I pushed
it away.

LIVERPOOL

S.S TITA

The *Titanic* was sinking faster now, as she began to take on more and more sea water. The lifeboats began rowing away from her so they wouldn't be sucked down as well.

The *Titanic's* nose dipped underwater and her tilt suddenly became much worse. On the deck I could see people – hundreds of people – trying to climb the increasing slope to get to the rear of the ship.

There was a loud shriek of steam as the cold water of the ocean flooded into the engine room.

The *Titanic* was screaming.

She tilted more and her rear lifted out of the water. Her three giant propellers hung in the air. Out of water they looked ugly and strangely awkward.

I knew there were only moments left.

People were jumping from the deck, plunging into the freezing sea below.

She tilted still further and there was a deafening crash as the engines broke loose and fell the entire length of the ship smashing through all the walls.

For a few seconds, the *Titanic* hung balanced with her nose underwater and her propellers pointed towards the sky.

Then there was another explosion as cold sea water finally engulfed the hot engines. There was a terrible sound of straining metal as her body buckled, then ripped itself in two.

"She's breaking in half!"

Her front half slipped under the surface of the ocean and disappeared.

Around us, people were crying and those thrown into the freezing water were struggling to reach the lifeboats.

The *Titanic's* rear half floated by itself for a moment longer, then it too slid silently under the surface.

The dark ocean quickly closed over her, leaving no trace at all.

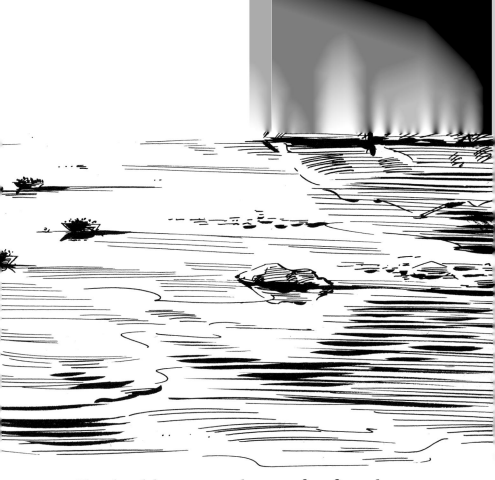

She had been our home for five days.
Now, suddenly, the *Titanic* was gone and
the ocean seemed a huge and empty
place. Our tiny lifeboats were alone in
the night, lost in the middle of the
Atlantic Ocean.

I put my hand in my pocket and touched the sketch Mr Andrews had given me - all that was left of the unsinkable *Titanic*.

"She's gone."

Chapter 5

Some of the lifeboats were overloaded with people, so they rowed towards those with empty spaces in them – like ours.

"How many can you take?" shouted the rower.

"Room for six."

Two small children, three women and one man were passed into our boat. I looked to see if I could see my friend Eva in any of the nearby lifeboats, but it was too dark.

Everybody sat quietly,
shivering and shocked.

I looked up and saw
a shooting star. Then
another. I had never
seen the sky so clear.

Without warning,
the stars suddenly
disappeared as a huge
floating mass blotted
them out.

"Another iceberg!"

From out of the
darkness, a huge
iceberg was drifting
towards us. Its
craggy white bulk
dwarfed our boat.

"Row. Quickly!"

The iceberg that sank the *Titanic* was not alone. It was just one of a whole iceberg field – and we were adrift right in the middle of it.

As dawn broke, I could see that icebergs surrounded us on all sides like gigantic mountain ranges.

The sea was beginning to get rougher. The swell made our boat bob up and down, but worse, it felt like there was a storm on the way.

The jagged peaks of the icebergs floated across each other making strange patterns on the horizon.

Then I saw a small black dot. A black dot with smoke coming from it.

"Look!"

There was a ship carefully steering its way through the icebergs towards us.

"Thank God."

We hadn't known it, but a ship called the *Carpathia* had heard the *Titanic's* distress signal and had been steaming towards us all night.

In the lifeboats, all heads turned to watch our rescue ship approach.

To get on board the *Carpathia*, people had to climb up a 15-metre rope ladder up the side of the ship.

It was even worse for children. I was put into a canvas bag with just my head sticking out and then winched up the side of the ship! Like everyone else, I screamed all the way up.

Waiting for us in the ship's dining room were warm blankets and hot drinks and hot food.

Through the crowd of survivors I caught sight of a familiar face.

It was Eva.

I started to go over to her, but mother pulled me back. Eva was clinging to her own mother and she was crying.

"I don't think her father is with them," said mother simply, and left it at that.

Later they pinned up a list of
survivor's names. Underneath it said:
"SURVIVORS – 706
LOST AT SEA – 1502"
We were shown to a cabin and given
dry clothes. As I changed, I found Mr
Andrews' sketch in my pocket.

I unfolded it. The sea water had
smudged the ink, turning it into a sticky,
black mess.

I screwed it up and threw it over the
side into the rough water churned up by
the *Carpathia's* propellers.

It floated for a second then disappeared.